# Earth Rejoicing

## Collection of Poetry

### By Kathie Trujillo Nye

RoseDog Books
585 Alpha Drive
Suite 103
Pittsburgh, PA 15238
Visit our website at *www.rosedogbookstore.com*

ISBN: 978-1-63867-451-1
eISBN: 978-1-63867-547-1

# Earth Rejoicing

## Collection of Poetry

# Earth Rejoicing

As I stood on the pier that summer day
Peacefully gazing across the sea,
Suddenly, a thousand diamonds appeared,
Twinkling and dancing upon the bay.

Then, gradually, the sea brought forth a harmony of praise,
A chorus of excitement, erupting into pure joy!
Every molecule rejoiced in the warmth of the sun
And its glorious, light-filled rays.

How blessed am I.
Have you ever wondered:
Is the earth alive,
And does it possess a spirit as you and I?

By Katherine "Kathie" Trujillo Nye

# Visions of Eternity

Happiness is a choice, I'm told.
But, what if I'm grieved and can't abide.
Should I give up the fight and wish to die?

Come away in spirit…dream.
The curtains of time are parted to view a golden sunset
    bathed on a mountainside.
Then, hear the gentle lapping of the surf as it rises and falls with the tide.

Before I awake from my vision, my sorrows have melted away, indeed.
And I glimpse the warmth of my future home,
    with friendships that are to be.


By Katherine "Kathie" Trujillo Nye

# My Childhood Friend

He was my childhood neighbor and friend.
But his family moved away.
Oh, how I wish that they could have stayed.
At first, we kept in touch.
But, I have not heard of him 'till this day.

Years later, my mind drifted to thoughts of Danny.
What had become of my childhood friend?
Then, I received a message from his brother so far away.
The message read:  Did you hear?
Danny died just yesterday.
Coincidence?


Katherine "Kathie" Trujillo Nye

# Surfing Memories of Youth

As I step in the ocean with my board,
Beautiful swells rise which I must climb,
And I glide over the crest to the other side.
Not crushed—I was fortunate to survive!

Then, another light-filled wave in the distance appears.
I paddle furiously and lasso that wave
And manage to stand up—what a thrill to arise!
Being hurled toward the shore in a mystical way
    is a sensation that I cannot describe.

While surfing the wave, I am enchanted to see
    the beauty of the green hills that jut down to the sea.
Anointed with water of the sea, this sacred experience
    purifies me.

It is a dream that I repeat, repeat, repeat.


By Katherine "Kathie" Trujillo Nye

# Meeting Aspens

Cruising along the Alpine Loop, my breath was taken away to suddenly
  see a grove of sunlit aspen trees.
Leaves, looking like bright, golden coins, shimmered and fluttered in
the breeze.
Listening closely, I thought I should hear them gently chime.
The inner-city, Los Angeles girl had never seen white-barked aspen trees,
  and the meeting was sublime.

This enchanting scene was silhouetted by a clear, azure sky.
In the moment, it seemed that time stood still for eternity.
So, I'll keep this memory hidden safely in my heart until I die.
The world may take away my earthly wealth, but no one can steal this memory.


Katherine "Kathie" Trujillo Nye

# A Child in the Old Port Town of San Pedro

As an impressionable child,
I lie in my bed,
Reflecting on the dismal, foggy night.

I was being lulled to sleep by the sound of foghorns.
Years later, I'm saddened to think that the world moved on
    from a sound so comforting — yet forlorn.


By Katherine "Kathie" Trujillo Nye

# Memories of Lost Lake

Lost Lake has a unique spirit.
The sky and clouds testify to this.
With dense, pine forests that reach for the shore,
  this sanctuary's beauty cannot be ignored.

Mt. Hood stands sentinel from above, guarding its domain.
It is cloaked in snow year-round, with an exquisite pyramidal shape.
The majestic mountain is mirrored on the lake.
Its reflection cannot be diminished by my passing canoe's calm wake.

As I walk the path that encircles this serene lake,
  the peace is punctuated by the song of a sparrow.
Surely, the sparrow delights to own this space.

The setting sun, upon Mt. Hood, is embraced.
It returns the favor by giving back a pinkish glow.
While gazing upon this scene, a cozy campfire soothes my burdened soul.
And I think to myself: While lingering here, no sadness can I know.


Katherine "Kathie" Trujillo Nye

# Who Was That Special Woman?

She exuded a serenity that seemed to radiate from within.
Such beauty, for me, was hard to comprehend.

Her nose was rather prominent,
But it appeared lovely to me.
For it represented an inner strength that not everyone could see.

Her hair was a dull, brown shade.
Yet, it was soft, and seemed, before my eyes, to grow.
It reflected the compassion and kindness of her soul.
Her being was full of light and truth, with a luminous glow.

Who was that special woman — will I ever know?


Katherine "Kathie" Trujillo Nye

# Wisdom

As a girl of thirteen, I thought I knew what love was.
Being attracted to a boy was all that was necessary.
He had black hair, green eyes and was tall.
Did this have anything to do with love at all?
But, was he also kind, charming and interesting?

What did I know?
Year later, I learned to love wisely, beautifully.
I learned to love my man's soul.


Katherine "Kathie" Trujillo Nye

# Compassion

You ask how I knew of your sorrow
   that plunged you into despair.
Why should I react or care?

I only know the spirit whispered to me of your pain.

Oh, but you and I have both been blessed.
You were comforted and captured your passion.
I earned the gift of compassion.


By Katherine "Kathie" Trujillo Nye

# Where Did I Come From?

As a child, I looked up at the night sky —
Beneath a canopy of white stars,
I wondered: Where did I come from?

When did my spirit birth begin?
Had my spirit always been here
Or was I from a higher sphere?
Where did I come from?

Katherine "Kathie" Trujillo Nye

# Teenage Love

I didn't know you were dating him and that your love for him had grown.
I only know that he came to my door,
Professing his love evermore.

Why be angry with me?
It is he who committed by giving you the ring.

Saddened that our friendship came to an end,
I wonder: In the eternities, will we be friends again?


Katherine "Kathie" Trujillo Nye

# Chasing the Seal

Standing on the beach…
    suddenly, a little seal popped up, bobbing in the waves.
The seal looked at me, I looked at it, and, soon, our eyes did meet.

Never letting me out of its sight, it swam and beckoned me, it seemed,
    to follow along.

I ran and struggled to keep up with my friend—and stay on track.
The seal in the sea and I on the shore…
The seal liked me, and I liked it right back.


Katherine "Kathie" Trujillo Nye

# The Awakening

As the sun steals across the sky, leafy shadows appear
   silhouetted on the wall outside my bedroom window.
At two years of age, I awakened to a world I'd never known.

I looked forward to seeing the shadows again.
In time, I thought of them as my friends.
As summer turned to fall, they completely disappeared.
My two-year old mind wondered why my friendships came to
   An end.


Katherine "Kathie" Trujillo Nye

9 781638 674511